Driving from the Backseat

Ronnie L. Bryant

Copyright © 2019 Ronnie L. Bryant
All rights reserved.
ISBN: 13: 978-1-0908-6159-7

Reviews / Endorsements

"In *Driving from the Back Seat*, Ronnie Bryant asks the all-important question of Why. Why have you chosen this career path? In the subsequent chapters, we learn from his experience about, patience, leadership, managing expectations, and being true to yourself when working with a non-profit board. His key points provide a framework and 'survival guide' for working in a non-profit world."

Dean Whittaker, CEcD, President/CEO of Whittaker Associates, Inc.

"*Driving from the Back Seat* is a must-read for CEOs (and aspiring CEOs) of economic development organizations and other nonprofits. Ronnie L. Bryant's management wisdom is invaluable to anyone interested in building positive engagement among their board members and other community stakeholders. It is especially relevant in this era of public misunderstanding and scrutiny of our field. This book shares lessons learned during a lifetime of experience through thoughtful advice and real examples from deep within the trenches of leadership."

Amy Holloway, President and CEO, Avalanche Consulting

"Ronnie Bryant's DRIVING FROM THE BACKSEAT should be mandatory reading for all CEO's of economic development organizations. It's not just a survival guide but a guide to success in working with non-profit boards, business leaders and stakeholders. Ronnie sprinkles golden nuggets of wisdom in every chapter that is gleaned from many years of experience. This is not just a book that is read and sits on a shelf but a reference manual for non-profit CEO's to use when leading and navigating through ambiguous and challenging environments."

Craig J. Richard, CEcD, FM, President/CEO of Tampa Hillsborough EDC

"Bryant has developed a comprehensive and crafted toolkit that belongs on the shelves of all economic development leaders' libraries. This book is brimming with advice and motivation, notably, for leaders to look inward and evaluate their personal priorities before acting externally to address community priorities. It emphasizes the importance of maintaining a personal commitment to and belief in one's organization, as Bryant poignantly reflects on the consequences if this passion falters. Bryant utilizes the analogy of "driving from the backseat" to illustrate the personal wisdom he has gained from more than 30 years navigating the nonprofit environment, encouraging self-reflection in his readers. He reaffirms the importance for economic development leaders to position themselves as community servants to ensure their longevity and success with their organizations. A must-read for community leaders wishing to achieve excellence and longevity in their positions."

Jeffrey A. Finkle, CEcD, President/CEO of International Economic Development Council (IEDC)

"Who am I? Why am I here? What should I do now? In *Driving from the Backseat*, Ronnie Bryant answers these three questions succinctly but thoroughly. He demonstrates an uncanny sense of self-awareness as he takes the reader through three decades of hands on experience in the field of nonprofit organization leadership. Give it a good read and you'll understand why these three questions are so important to your career advancement and success."

Rick Weddle, Executive Director of The Site Selectors Guild

"Read it, read it again and then reread it. Each time you'll find valuable nuggets to enhance your personal and organizational success. Great insight for folks just entering the non-profit world and refreshing ideas for the seasoned practitioner. I wish I had read this book twenty-five years ago."

Tim Chase CEcD, FM, National Sales Manager, ProTRACKPlus /Practice Leader, Quality Metrics

CONTENTS

Reviews / Endorsements		Page 3
1.	Who am I and why am I here?	Page 6
2.	Am I a Thought Leader or a Servant Leader?	Page 10
3.	I can see clearly now	Page 13
4.	What a difference a day makes	Page 15
5.	Driving from the backseat	Page 18
6.	Potential for Civic Lobotomy	Page 21
7.	Managing someone else's expectations	Page 23
8.	The Illusive Unanimous Affirmation	Page 26
9.	Being true to yourself	Page 29
10.	Honesty– To Be or Not to Be	Page 31
11.	It's not a job. It's a lifestyle	Page 33
12.	Realistic vs. Unrealistic Tenure	Page 36
13.	"Hail! Hail! The gang's all here"	Page 39
14.	You are your brother's keeper	Page 41
Summary		Page 43
Quotes		Page 44
Key Chapter Takeaways		Page 46
About the Author		Page 50

Chapter One

Who am I and Why am I Here?

"Risk more than others think is safe, care more than others think is wise, dream more than others think is practical, expect more than others think is possible." **Claude Bissell**

It's not a coincidence that the first chapter of this survival guide addresses who you are and why you've chosen this profession. It's imperative that you understand what motivates you to want the position and if you have the unique skill-set required to be good at it. There is passion that is needed as well as skill. Therefore, you need both, the heart and the head.

This process to determine if you have the heart and the head starts with a reflective evaluation of yourself. What do you really know about your motivations and how those motivations have evolved over the years of your work experience? In an organization, regardless of size, the board of directors is responsible for general direction and governance. However, the ultimate responsibility for execution rests with the CEO. The organization's mission, stakeholders, employees, etc., demand a unique external level of focus and understanding. But, that external focus must not precede an understanding of the unique skills that you must possess to be effective and maximize your chances of survival.

CEOs are hired to lead an organization, not just manage it. Therefore, your mindset should be one of providing leadership, not just maintenance. Be a "thermostat" that sets the room temperature instead of a thermometer that measures a room's temperature. An effective CEO sets the environmental temperature by leading, guiding and mentoring, as opposed to reacting to norms established by others. As with a thermostat, the CEO must be aware of the environment and willing to make adjustments in order to sustain effectiveness.

Not-for-profit CEOs have a significantly different level of expectations than our for-profit counterparts. There are many more stakeholders (bosses) involved in governance, and the goals and objectives are not as clearly defined as in the for-profit world. The for-profit CEO can, to a certain extent, be very selective regarding how broad a net the organization can cast in defining its stakeholder groups. The not-for-profit has very little overall discretion or control with the level of engagement from its board of directors, partner organizations, the media, community groups and the general public.

The ambiguity of such an environment can be frustrating, and eventually detrimental if the CEO is not aware of the need to address nuances of not only individual groups, but the individuals within each group. You find yourself much more engaged in subjective conversations as opposed to conversations that have an objective nature. For example, you might have a conversation with your treasurer about the color of the wallpaper in the board room, as opposed to a matter related to the organization's finances. The CEO must be very aware of his/her tolerance for allowing this level of input from others, whether welcomed or not, and to what extent it will influence decision making and your general style of leadership.

There is a direct correlation between the success of the CEO's tenure and his/her understanding of how performance is evaluated. The ambiguity of the environment, as discussed above, leads directly to ambiguity in the evaluation process. There is a tendency for stakeholder inputs to be more of a subjective, emotional nature than what would be perceived as logical. Understand that your tenure will be determined around how well you are liked, not by how good you are at your job. Even when there are clearly defined quantitative goals for the organization as well as the CEO, there is a level of subjectivity that can be more influential in the process. Also, board and officer turnover results in evolving players as well as evolving expectations.

It's imperative that you identify the "points of influence" that will ultimately determine the results of your performance evaluation. These points of influence are individuals who will formally or informally provide input at a level that will factor significantly into the results. These individuals usually stand out because of the obvious influence they have over the others in the room. They are the ones who lead with their opinion and the others will tend to follow. Your understanding of the motivations of these identified influencers is crucial to the success of your tenure and ultimate survival.

Your approach towards determining your interest and motivations must be thorough. The ultimate goal in understanding yourself relative to job performance is understanding what is important to you and what you are good at doing. Self-assessment tools such as Myers-Briggs, DiSC or Strengths Finder, can be used to gain better insight into oneself. But by the time you are ready to assume the role of CEO, it is hoped that you would have achieved a high level of self-awareness including your tolerance level for various types of leadership.

There also should be a correlation between your needs and the needs of the organization. Speak openly with your stakeholder leadership and have candid conversations with your predecessor to develop a correlation. Open communication with key leadership should lead to identifying their level of understanding of the mission of the organization, as well as an understanding of their role and your role. Have your eyes wide-open and sincerely objectively evaluate yourself as you attempt to match those needs with the needs of the organization.

Another area of awareness that addresses the questions, "Who am I?" and "Why am I here?" is work-life balance. A lot has been written about the importance of having work/life balance, the pluses of getting it right, and minuses of not getting it right. Although most opinions lean towards work being secondary to non-work activities, some would argue that non-work activities, including family, friends, hobbies, etc., are secondary to building a successful career, as well as being an effective leader. I am personally aware of the severe impact of not balancing work and non-work activities. A healthy environment outside of work directly impacts your ability to perform at the expected level while at work. Enjoying the satisfaction of the internal peace received from personal relationships, hobbies, etc., enables you to focus while at work, meet the expectations of your stakeholders, and master the responsibilities of leadership. It's imperative that you understand the impact your job has on your health, family and overall quality of life. These work/life balance decisions we make along the way can take their toll and often become apparent after it's too late to take corrective action.

KEY TAKEWAY:

Serving as a CEO for a not-for-profit organization comes with unique challenges. Be prepared to spend more time communicating with influencers and internal stakeholders than you may have done in previous roles.

Be proactive in setting clear objectives for your performance and that of your organization.

Chapter Two

Am I a Thought Leader or a Servant Leader?

"A leader… is like a shepherd. He stays behind the flock, letting the nimblest go out ahead, whereupon the others follow, not realizing that all along they are being directed from behind." **Nelson Mandela**

One of the most enduring qualities of a successful CEO is the ability to provide unquestionable leadership. In every organization I've worked with and in every community I've worked in, there's an insatiable desire for someone to rise to the top and take charge. The desire is evident in the way communities recruit not-for-profit leadership. Executive search firms are charged with not only identifying candidates with the prerequisite experience, but also with the demeanor that conveys, "I've got this!"

Now for the tricky part. As CEO, you possess the skills and experience, you've passed the, "I've got this!" test and you have a community that wants what you have to offer. It appears to be a perfect environment, but it can quickly evolve into the storm after the calm. The manner in which you define and execute your leadership style will determine the quality and length of your tenure. My personal approach is to understand the distinction between being a thought leader and a servant leader. Also, I now believe that the two are not mutually exclusive and at times may be practiced in tandem.

Following up on the thermostat/thermometer analogy discussed earlier, think of a thought leader as the thermostat and the servant leader as more of the thermometer. Thought leaders set the pace, drive the discussion and sell the vision. They are driven by a combination of influence, experience and personality. They convey a sense of confidence that meets the expectations of stakeholders. Again, "I've got this!"

On the other hand, servant leadership is more geared towards stepping back and being more aware of the emotional "temperature" of the situation. Servant leaders are more likely to allow others to be much more involved in setting the pace and driving the agenda. This is not to infer an abdication of responsibilities, but just a more passive approach to leadership.

Maximum sustainability and effectiveness is achieved by balancing thought leadership with servant leadership. They are not mutually exclusive. The balance is achieved by being aware of the situation and the personalities involved. Being able to analyze the situation very quickly and develop a strategy to minimize the tension and solve the issue. You walk into the board room prior to a meeting to discuss a contentious issue, and you see small groups of stakeholders huddling and mumbling about the issue at hand. Based on your presumed knowledge of the leaders of each pocket, it's incumbent upon the CEO to guide the discussion by ensuring that each side has an opportunity to make their case, as well as hear the opposing positions. It is very important to take charge and guide the group to a solution that YOU can live with, as well as one that compliments the mission of the organization.

Balancing thought and servant leadership is more art than science, and it's an art form that's not optional. Another way of describing this balance is to think of "toggling" – switching from one form of leadership to the other and understanding which side of your brain is more dominate for each style. The left side of the brain is analytic and therefore geared towards thought leadership. The right side is emotional and would be more dominate with servant leadership. It's imperative that you are able to capture the emotional intelligence in the room and balance your engagement with each individual based on that intelligence. Remember, your stakeholders are looking for leadership, but your survival is directly correlated to how you apply such leadership.

One of my most effective leadership strategies is to develop a "bottoms up" leadership style. Being an effective leader of a regional economic development organization is a difficult job, to say the least. The level of difficulty is multiplied when your stakeholders and other constituencies believe that your leadership style is dictatorial, or "top down", and they are expected to, "fall in line." In fact, the difficulty will only increase in future years as the millennial workforce does not support organizational structures or management with a top down, command and control style.

Strategically positioning yourself as support (servant leadership), while also providing guidance (thought leadership) ensures a more collaborative and productive working environment. Long-term goodwill and support is secured when you empower your leadership, partners, other stakeholders and staff to provide a level of input that satisfies their need for substantive engagement but allows you the opportunity to provide supportive leadership. Therefore, "Driving from the Backseat"!

KEY TAKEAWAY:

As the CEO of a non-profit organization your leadership encompasses two strategic approaches - that of the dynamic thought leader and that of a servant leader. Your thought leadership must embody strength, vision, and drive, while your servant leadership must embrace and navigate divergent positions and personalities to move forward toward collective success.

Chapter Three

I Can See Clearly Now....

"Good business leaders create a vision, articulate the vision, passionately own the vision, and relentlessly drive it to completion." **Jack Welch**

One of the most critical mistakes a not-for-profit leader can make is to establish an operating environment that's based on a series of activities but lacks a clear vision and identifiable direction for the organization. This is comparable to a band leader directing its members to start playing, without first identifying the musical composition to be played. Organizational management consultant Simon Sinek would characterize this start as the "Why, how and what?"

The Jack Welsh quote clearly identifies the four components of visionary leadership: 1) creation, 2) articulation, 3) ownership and 4) execution. This is a natural expectation of leadership, partners, stakeholders and the community at large, and is necessary to maximize the probability of a sustainable and effective tenure.

Creation of the vision is the result of developing consensus among those with a vested interest (i.e. leadership, partners, stakeholders and the community at large) and ensuring their commitment towards execution. This step involves facilitating discussions at every level and providing the group an opportunity to provide input relative to the direction of the organization, as well as articulate their expectations for defining success. Remember, people want to be led and not be told what to do. This inclusionary buy-in can be accomplished through focus groups, small gatherings and individual meetings. The accumulated data is now synthesized and integrated with your experience and intuition. The plan, which should have a three to five-year life span, must be flexible and open to modifications as needed.

The **articulation** process occurs after the collected data and stakeholder input is compiled into a <u>strategic plan</u> that clearly details how the visionary expectations will be realized. It is imperative that the strategic plan directly correlates with the input received from the creation process, includes realistic activities, and is affordable. Your strategic plan becomes the foundation for all future activities of the organization.

Your **ownership** of the visionary plan, in my opinion, is what will separate winners from losers. Earlier we discussed conveying an "I've got this!" attitude. The intent is not to appear arrogant but position yourself as being a confident leader who has developed a consensus-driven vision and is willing to take the necessary steps to clearly articulate the vision. Although the plan was created by consensus, this now is your plan and based on your vision, and you must passionately <u>own it</u> and encourage others to accept it.

The final piece is **execution** or putting the plan in action. Remember, the plan was developed with consensus, has been clearly articulated, has identified ownership, and must now be put to action. The infrastructure (i.e. staffing, budget, etc.) of your organization should be developed to match the requirements of the visionary plan. Now, the goal is to ensure that under your leadership the objectives of the plan are realized, and through consistent communication and opportunities for engagement your stakeholders are supportive and reasonably pleased with the program.

This has now become your visionary plan. Every ounce of your being should now be focused on its successful execution. You are the band leader and must ensure that every member of the band clearly understands their individual role and how their involvement impacts the plan's successful execution. Based on your understanding of the skill set of each individual "band member," it's your responsibility to ensure that everyone knows their role and executes appropriately. Ed Morrison, Economic Policy Advisor for Purdue Center for Regional Development, describes this concept as "Strategic Doing," the development of new networks for organizational success.

KEY TAKEAWAY:

It is imperative that you establish a clear vision for what success looks like for your organization. The vision is your roadmap and guiding star as you drive the road to reaching your goals. You must get your stakeholders on your 'vision bus' from the start and then move ahead with your tactical plan and execution.

Chapter Four

What a difference a day makes…

"Be patient with yourself. Self-growth is tender, it's holy ground. There's no greater investment." **Steven Covey**

"Patience is the ability to idle your motor when you feel like stripping your gears." **Barbara Johnson**

If there is one thing I've learned over the years that I still struggle with, it's the distinction between reaction and response. An emotional response to an action that you perceive detrimental to your organization, or even to you personally, can cause concern among your supporters as well as long-term damage to relationships. A more measured and methodical process for addressing issues provides a level of confidence and positions you as a mature and responsible leader.

As the leader of your organization, it's almost impossible for you to be able to make a personal public statement. For example, if you determine that a piece of legislation is detrimental to your mission or your community, providing a non-vetted, emotional reactive comment can cause substantial harm. You are perceived as speaking on behalf of your organization and therefore must be patient and follow a process of engaging leadership for a more measured response.

Every action does not require an immediate reaction. Some situations improve when and if you allow them to "simmer." There are also times when you must allow a perceived detrimental action to just dissolve. Patience is "the capacity to accept or tolerate delay, trouble, or suffering without getting angry or upset." A reactive emotional response, which can be rooted in the right side of the brain, clearly defies the logic of patience. Whereas a measured left-brain approach to addressing an issue has the highest probability of resulting in satisfactory results.

As leaders, we have an inherit desire to be perceived as strong, decisive and being able to get in front of an issue. The last thing we want is to be thought of as being weak or indecisive and not being able to take a stand without "testing the direction of the wind." This feeling is ego driven and is extremely dangerous. An incorrect response can not only damage your credibility but has the potential of attracting more attention to the perceived detrimental action than otherwise would have resulted if you did nothing.

Remember, think long and be patient. We are competing in a marathon, not a sprint. Every decision you make impacts your sustainability and ability to have a successful tenure. "Always, measure three times and cut once."

KEY TAKEAWAY:

Remember you are the 'brand' for your organization, especially when it comes to taking a public stand and/or making public comments. Learn to carefully consider the impact of your words and know when and how to respond on issues, both internally and externally. The most successful leaders have on-going professional communication training.

Chapter Five

Driving from the backseat...

"A leader takes people where they want to go. A great leader takes people where they don't necessarily want to go, but ought to be."
Rosalynn Carter

It's no coincidence that this chapter shares the same title as the book. The concept of "driving from the backseat" is not only the central theme of this book, but it is also one of the most significant topics we will discuss.

The analogy of an automobile with a driver behind the steering wheel, but with someone else in the backseat controlling the movements of the vehicle, is the perfect metaphor for this concept. Understanding the nuances and mastering the associated techniques will create an environment for organizational excellence, as well as provide substantial job security. The first step to receiving your "driver's license" is revisiting the individual emotional intelligence of your core leadership. Core leadership can be defined as your organization's Executive Committee, its officers, or a smaller less formal group. Regardless of how they are defined relative to the direction of the organization, these are the individuals with the most influence. In other words, they are in charge. With each member of this group, you must develop an intrinsic understanding of their behavior as well as their expectations of you and the organization. This is accomplished by spending as much one-on-one time together as possible. Identify and create opportunities for formal or informal "quality time." The goal is not to just hang out, but to really get to know the individual and allow them get to know you to some extent. This leads us to our next step.

In allowing a member of the core group to get to know you, your goal is to convey a sense of confidence and trust that places you above any suspicion of having a personal agenda which might be contrary to <u>their own</u>. I would not consider it too bizarre or negative to assume that each of the core group members will have a personal agenda. Accept it and learn how to use it to your advantage. I'm not insinuating in any way that you be disingenuous, but this is business. Remember, your leadership group members are not your friends, they are your employers. You can play golf together, break bread or share a glass of wine, but at the end of the day, you work for them and they can and will terminate you if necessary.

Finally, the delicate part. How do you engage core leadership and ensure that their agenda is being realized, when your influence and leadership drives the organization? You must develop a true understanding of the individuals within the group, and they must trust you. You also must operate at a level of informational and technical transparency that validates you as a knowledgeable leader and not a threat to their collective or individual agendas.

This may sound difficult to achieve, but I've established a few techniques over the years. I've learned to never enter a planning or brainstorming session with a "blank slate." It's always better to give your leadership something to respond to. Develop parameters that you can live with and allow your leadership to provide input or tweak what you've provided. For example, when seeking approval for a budgetary item, always request more than you need. This allows the fiscally conservative member an opportunity to request and win a reduction while still providing you with what you need. If your original request prevails, you are now able to fund the effort, come in below budget and further validate yourself as a fiscally responsible leader.

As important as this concept is, and although it might be delicate, it does not have to be difficult. Your experience and confidence naturally position you as the leader, and your leadership's role is to provide you and the organization with strategic guidance and support. As clear as this may sound, remember that you're working with individuals who have day jobs and serving on your board is a part-time gig. Their focus is limited, as well as their total knowledge of the issues that affect the organization. Get to know them, understand their personal nuances, learn what resonates with them about your organization in order to turn them into ambassadors, and then work with them to keep the car in the middle of the road.

KEY TAKEAWAY:

As the CEO of a not-for-profit you must be the driving force, but in a way that engenders support for your leadership and your vision. The key is to build understanding, professional respect and support with your core leadership. Maintaining professional and, to a very measured extent, personal relationships- with a keen eye on any individual 'agendas' - will help you keep a steady hand on the backseat wheel.

Chapter Six

Potential for Civic Lobotomy

"Only to the extent that trustees give support when it is needed does the chief executive want a strong board." **Robert Greenleaf**

I always find it amazing how some board members, who are smart and successful in their day jobs, can enter our boardroom and totally act and react contrary to the way they would in their private domain. To better understand this conversion, I characterized it as "civic lobotomy." Something strange happens when a measured, methodical civic leader walk through the door of a boardroom and transforms into a decision maker who is either 1) insecure and reluctant or 2) impulsive and reactionary. This chapter will attempt to define the transformation for the sake of understanding it, as well as offer suggestions for you to stabilize the environment.

An ideal board or leadership group would be one that consists of individuals who are hand-picked and vetted for individual skills and personality traits. But in most cases boards consist of 1) business leaders with a personal interest in the organization's mission, 2) "volunteers" who are assigned to represent their respective companies, or 3) other leaders within the community with an interest in being involved. What results can be a "Bad News Bears" band of misfits whose effectiveness as a group will be determined by the ability of the CEO (coach) to mold them into a cohesive group.

We first must understand and appreciate that individual board members want to make a contribution to the governance of the organization but, unfortunately, may not fully comprehend how different policy decisions impact the overall execution of the mission. With all due respect, board members have other responsibilities which have a higher priority in their individual lives. It's very possible, unless you have other staff present, that you are the only person in the room whose full-time job is to be responsible for the organization. This makes you a powerful participant, because you control the information.

It's imperative that you provide a systematic method of presenting information that gives every member an opportunity to feel informed and empowered. Give them an opportunity to feel "smart." Receive buy-in prior to the meeting by connecting with targeted members to prepare for the ensuing discussion. Systematically communicate with your leadership and never allow them to be surprised in an open session. For those who are insecure and reluctant, they should be nurtured and given an opportunity to participate with authority. For those who tend to be impulsive or reactionary, they should be presented with parameters of issues at hand and given an opportunity to provide constructive input based on their respective experiences and expertise.

Remember, in most cases board members want to be involved and want to provide constructive input. Earlier we discussed emotional intelligence, which is your understanding of the individual nuances. Treat your leadership as individuals and not as a collective group. Your goal is to provide a level of leadership that makes this group an asset, not a liability. Utilizing systematic nurturing and consistently providing relevant information, you now can transform the group into a cohesive, informed governance body.

KEY TAKEAWAY:

One of your key responsibilities in being an effective CEO is to clearly understand the individuals in your core leadership, including why they committed to being a director and their view of where they see the organization going and why. In addition, you have the critical role of providing clear, consistent information so that they may feel fully informed and enabled to successfully carry out their roles as board members.

Chapter Seven
Managing someone else's expectations

"The world isn't interested in the storms you encountered, but whether or not you brought in the ship." **Raul Armesto**

Over the years, I'm always amazed at the number of stakeholders who have opinions and expectations regarding the direction of the organization, as well as my leadership of the organization. A few years ago, a good friend and mentor of mine, Rick Weddle, shared his thoughts with me regarding economic developers being in the business of "meeting expectations." Since that conversation, I have come to believe that Rick is correct, and that not-for-profit leadership is the practice of managing someone else's expectations as well as your own. Leadership has its collective expectation of the successful execution of the mission of the organization, but the more difficult responsibility is understanding and managing the expectations of your individual board members, as well as other stakeholders.

How you balance your execution with the input provided by others is directly correlated to the effectiveness and longevity of your tenure. It can be extremely frustrating to leave a meeting with what you believe is consensus regarding an issue or policy directive, and then return to your email inbox and find that several participants have thoughts that they were not willing to share with the full group. In most cases the additional input is contrary to the presumed consensus. It's also not inconceivable to be informed that the presumed consensus should never be acted upon. The impulsive reaction is to respond that the matter was thoroughly vetted, and a direction was agreed upon, therefore, the matter is closed. NOT!!

Situations such as these test your leadership savvy. You now must balance the expectations of a few, presumably influential individuals, with the results of an official documented directive. This is truly more art than science. One thought is to reconvene the group and offer new evidence for additional discussion. This might work, if the new information is truly substantive and has the potential of improving the original meeting outcome, as well as aligning with your execution parameters. Therefore, if reconvening is logistically feasible, it might be worth the effort.

But, in most cases, the additional post-meeting input is subjective and adds very little if any value to the outcome. Your mission now is to convince the post-meeting contributor that what was decided upon is in the best interest of the organization, and what they are proposing, although relevant, at least in their mind, cannot be inserted now, if ever. This is where emotional intelligence is so important. Emotional intelligence is the ability to identify and manage your own emotions and the emotions of others. For starters, you should not be surprised that a stakeholder would not agree with the rest of the group. Remember, your understanding of the individual nuances of your leadership is crucial. There should always be conversations prior to the meeting with targeted individuals to hopefully avert an unwarranted intrusion either during the meeting or post-meeting.

Identifying whom to target is not an exact science and should enlist the collective thoughts of other staff members as well as members of the leadership group that you know are onboard. These questions must be asked: 1) "Who is most likely to have strong opinions regarding this issue?" and 2) "Who is the best person to have a conversation with them?" Again, this is an area where <u>emotional intelligence</u> and your intellectual and political savvy combine to smooth what could evolve into troubled waters. Getting it right assures you of a smooth implementation of the proposed policy, settling of any contentious issues, as well as strengthened personal credibility with your leadership.

When it comes to committee or board votes, the minimum acceptable result is 51 percent in favor of the position that you support. We all desire to have as much broad support as possible, but we shouldn't allow that desire to cost us precious time and/or in some cases credibility. Spending too much effort on the negative hardliners, in addition to lost time, can erode or at the very least negatively impact, your credibility with the rest of the committee or board. Allowing yourself to be forced to defend, instead of presenting your position, has the potential to dilute your position or have it substantially modified due to being forced into a superfluous compromise. Identify the negative hardliners and work to neutralize them as early as possible.

KEY TAKEAWAY:

As the leader of your organization you will have a myriad of stakeholders who have their own constituencies, opinions, agendas and biases. It will take your skills in emotional intelligence and collaborative engagement to bring alignment for the vision you have set. It is important that you proactively communicate with these decision makers in order to drive cohesion and cooperation.

Chapter Eight

The Illusive Unanimous Affirmation

"When I look in the mirror each morning, I accept the fact that at least 30% of the contacts I make will not be in agreement with me." **Ronnie Bryant**

In the previous chapter, we discussed meeting the expectations of your leadership and other stakeholders. We all have the intrinsic desire to have our thoughts and ideas accepted by others. But unfortunately, regardless of your political savviness or how charming your personality might be, you will find unanimous affirmation to be illusive. It is virtually impossible to satisfy every member of your stakeholder sphere. Unanimous affirmation is not an objective you can achieve, nor should it be an objective that you should extend valuable time attempting to achieve.

We have spent a substantial amount of time detailing the importance of self-confidence, being prepared and being knowledgeable regarding the subject at hand. If you are a master of the subject matter, you are not subject to whims and sometimes self-serving injections of others. You should be very comfortable asserting your beliefs and boldly discounting those around you whose opinions are not fact-based and provide no serious merit to the discussion.

I learned a long time ago, that it's important to quickly identify the stakeholders that truly have sincere motives and can add substance to the discussion. Spending time and effort with those individuals add value to the discussion and is a good use of your time. Spending time with individuals that provide no positive value, I call them "negative hardliners", is a waste of time. Now, please understand, in the name of job security, you shouldn't blatantly discount a member of your leadership, or a stakeholder. I've learned that one of the most effective techniques for quieting a negative hardliner, is to have the position that you support presented by an influential member of your leadership. It's very unlikely that a negative hardliner will challenge a sound position, especially in a nefarious manner, if it's known early that the position is supported by the influential member.

It took years for me to get comfortable with not having unanimous support or acceptance, which is expressed in the quote above. In fact, I now truly believe that if you need unanimous affirmation to feel comfortable, of if you desire to have a group hug after every meeting, you're either in the wrong business, the wrong position, or both. Your ability to fulfill the mission and objectives of your organization should not be dependent on you feeling loved and trying to make everybody happy. Accept the fact that there will always be "road kill" and you are not responsible for cleaning it up. Your political savviness and engaging approach can help mitigate the negative impact, but there is no guarantee that the hardliners will be happy. So be it. Sometimes you have to let the chips fall where they may.

When it comes to committee or board votes, the minimum acceptable result is 51 percent in favor of the position that you support. We all desire to have as much broad support as possible, but we shouldn't allow that desire to cost us precious time and, in some cases, credibility. Spending too much effort on the negative hardliners, in addition to lost time can erode, or at the very least negatively impact, your credibility with the rest of the committee or board. Allowing yourself to be forced to defend instead of presenting your position, has the potential to have your position diluted or substantially modified, due to being forced into a superfluous compromise. Identify the negative hardliners and work to neutralize them as early as possible.

KEY TAKEAWAY:

One of the keys to maintaining leadership is to remember that you are in the people business. Just as with public relations, you should spend the greater percentage of your time on solidifying relationships with your supporters and your 'middle of the roaders' rather than trying to pull the constant detractors to your side. As the old saying goes - "You can please some of the people all of the time, you can please all of the people some of the time, but you can't please all of the people all of the time".
Don't take it personally.

Chapter Nine

Being True to Yourself

"If you don't see yourself as a winner, then you cannot perform as a winner." **Zig Ziglar**

In my opinion, Hilary Hinton "Zig" Ziglar is one the greatest motivational speakers to have ever lived. His simple consistent message was that <u>you must believe in yourself</u>. In the not-for-profit environment, it's imperative that you unapologetically believe in yourself and the abilities that you bring to the position as chief executive officer. There is no room for doubt or second guessing. As we discussed earlier, you must be confident in your abilities, almost border-line arrogant, but short of being a narcissist.

In addition to believing in yourself, you also must believe in the mission of the organization that you are charged with leading. If you are not passionate about the mission, from my perspective, you have two choices; change the mission or change organizations. Every not-for-profit organization deserves to have a CEO that is passionate about its mission and fully dedicated to fulfilling the agreed upon objectives that will hopefully lead to success. The leadership and your staff deserve your passion. I would consider myself a hypocrite if I led an organization and was not fully onboard with the mission. It would be difficult for me to give 100 percent of my effort if I wasn't excited about what we are working to achieve. The combination of self-confidence and passion for the mission are inseparable. This valuable combination empowers you to give your all, which will lead to success and longevity with the organization.

It's not unheard of to be in a situation where you might have inherited a legacy mission that needs updating. It goes without saying, the organization's mission should be a consensus among leadership, stakeholders and in some cases the broader community. But your input and acceptance are imperative. You are charged with executing the mission and meeting its goals and objectives. Therefore, you must believe in the mission and see yourself as an extension of it. Whether you like it are not, if you are the public face of organization, you become synonymous with the mission within the community. It's to your advantage to be identified with a mission that you are passionate about and have the strongest possibility of accomplishing. Remember, you will be held accountable for its success or failure.

In addition to how you are perceived by your leadership, stakeholders and the broader community, relative to the mission, the team that you you're managing must see an unwavering support from you for what they've been asked to accomplish. Every aspect of your engagement is being monitored by your team. The culture of an organization is set at the top, and that culture emulates throughout each team member. If you want 100 percent engagement from your team, then you must also give 100 percent engagement. As stated earlier, if you are not totally bought into the mission, then I don't believe that it's possible for you to lead giving 100 percent, and therefore you will not receive 100 percent from your team. Your acceptance of the mission and your confidence towards successful execution, should be visibly unwavering to your leadership, stakeholders, community and team. It's what they deserve.

KEY TAKEAWAY:

Before ever stepping into the role of CEO it is nothing short of critical for you to believe with every fiber of your being in the mission, vision, values, purpose and potential of the organization. Anything short of that is a recipe for failure. Your stakeholders will know –sooner or later- if you do not fully have your heart and soul in what you do, whether you embody the organization's best interests, and if you truly are walking your talk when it comes to your commitment to their success.

Chapter Ten

Honesty – To Be or Not To Be...

"Integrity is doing the right thing, when no one is watching." **C.S. Lewis**

As I reflect on my career in a broader context of my life, I realize how important personal integrity is to success. Once I reached a point where I decided to, "lay all the chips on the table," in both my personal and professional life, a totally different perspective began to evolve. My thoughts became clearer and more internally satisfying. How I was projecting to an outside audience was no longer a concern because internally I felt that I was being totally truthful. My motivation evolved from being extrinsic to being intrinsic.

I have enjoyed the personal experience of vowing never to allow my personal integrity to come into question. You can't control the questions, but you have total control of the answer. I have chosen the quote above as my mantra for staying on track. Allowing such a mantra to guide my personal and professional career has produced benefits far exceeding my expectations. Allowing personal integrity to lead in all aspects of my life has given me an opportunity to have a balance which is directly correlated to professional success and organizational longevity. This is a heart issue for me, not a mind issue. It is driven by an emotional desire to do what's right and "let the chips fall where they may."

How your lifestyle is perceived within your community can impact your ability to successfully execute the activities for which you are responsible. The goal is to conduct your lifestyle in a manner that is above reproach. As I've stated earlier, I'm very comfortable with individuals or groups not agreeing with a policy issue or operational approach, but I am not comfortable having my personal integrity challenged. There are times when I have been accused of presenting misleading or outright erroneous information to make the case for my position. When, not if, this happens to you, it will be an opportunity to first reflect within your own heart that what you have presented is above reproach, and second provide a teachable moment to your audience. If you are confident that your integrity is in tack, you should have no problem pausing the conversation and letting those in the room know a little about you. This perception clarity will provide significant dividends as your relationship with your leadership, stakeholders and staff continue to evolve.

As I've stated, personal integrity is very important both in your personal and professional relationships, but you also have the right to expect those around you to subscribe to an acceptable level of truthful engagements and interactions. Again, the culture of an organization emanates from the top. You are responsible for creating an environment that is open and honest, and that starts with you. At no time should a team member feel that there are punitive consequences for being completely honest regarding a controversial situation. The goal is to receive accurate information to determine the best corrective action to take, not to punish the individual involved. There might be a need for a disciplinary conversation regarding the issue but placing blame and punishing a team member will not fix the problem.

KEY TAKEAWAY:

You, as CEO, drive the culture of an organization. Both personally and professionally you must represent –and Model - the highest standards of conduct and behavior. Maintaining unimpeachable ethical standards is not an option. Creating an environment that fosters transparency, collaboration and collegiately is under your purview. Your responsibility is to build and nurture your teams for a positive and productive working environment.

Chapter Eleven

It's not a job. It's a lifestyle

"The minute you stop making decisions to do your job and start making decisions to keep your job, you have become worthless." **Ronnie Bryant**

Each chapter of this book is preceded by a quote from someone famous or maybe not so famous. This is one of two chapters preceded by a quote attributed to me. I firmly believe that leading a not-for-profit organization is more than a job, it should be considered a lifestyle. If you are passionate about the mission (Chapter 9), you will soon determine that it's difficult to execute within a '9-to-5' environment. Operational success and organizational longevity are contingent upon you giving much more of yourself than what's available between 9:00 am and 5:00 pm.

It's imperative that you understand the difference between being "pig committed" versus being "chicken committed." Let me explain. Both the pig and chicken make a worthy contribution to a hearty breakfast; the pig contributes the bacon or ham and the chicken contributes the eggs. The pig's contribution is fatal, he gives his all. Where the chicken's contribution is not fatal and requires far less of a sacrifice. My belief is that we must be pig committed, willing to give it all, to achieve the success, we desire.

The passion you have for the mission, combined with your personal drive for success and longevity, demand that you give your all. This doesn't mean that you totally neglect a fulfilling work-life balance, but there must be a commitment to getting the job done. It's because of this fact that I believe that not-for-profit management is not for everyone. It takes a special individual to want to work in an environment with expectations from so many different directions (Chapter 7). It takes a special individual to want to work in an environment that at times can be thankless and, "damned if you do, damned if you don't." It takes a special individual to want to work in an environment where at times you must watch others take credit for your successes. It takes a special individual to want to work in an environment that at times you or your organization is publicly blamed for an infraction you didn't commit and had nothing to do with. Yet, your passion and commitment to the cause allows you to rise above the muddle and do what is necessary to get the job done. In other words, you become pig committed.

The attitude that you have developed becomes contagious. Your leadership, stakeholders and team members will soon recognize and appreciate your ability to rise above the muddle and do everything in your power to ensure the success of the organization and the execution of its mission. Those above will admire your commitment and value your confidence. Your team members will find joy working for a leader who is not only fully committed to the organization but leads with integrity and respect; a leader who values the importance of each employee and their contribution to the organization. Although, there is an expectation that they be pig committed also, it's easier to accept when such a commitment starts at the top.

Earlier I mentioned work-life balance. Jack Welch, the former CEO of General Electric, states that, "there's no such thing as work-life balance. There are work-life choices and you make them, and they have consequences." I believe that each of us must decide the priority of our life choices. The struggle for a balanced life is not new and it's different for each of us. According to Jim Schleckser, CEO of Inc. CEO Project, highly successful people measure themselves on seven key elements, Health, Family, Social, Financial, Business, Civic and Spiritual. Whatever your beliefs regarding work-life balance, you have choices to make and those choices will have consequences. Each CEO Project element referenced above should be important to each of us, but we must decide how important each will be.

KEY TAKEAWAY:

As the leader of your organization, with non-stop demands, duties and expectations, it is important to maintain your mental, physical and emotional health in order to succeed. That means thinking long and hard about how you will prioritize your life in terms of work and personal commitments. You must decide early on how you will create balance to prevent burnout. Preserving quality of life in and out of the workplace is important for success on both fronts.

Chapter Twelve

Realistic vs. Unrealistic Tenure

"You know it's time to leave when you began to believe something can't be done." **Michael Bloomberg**

Without a doubt, there is substantial turnover at the top of most not-for-profit organizations. I believe that turnover can be good for both the organization and in some cases the individual CEO. Being a change agent should be part of every not-for-profit leader's job description. We are recruited and hired to change and hopefully improve the performance of the organization. No one is recruited just to maintain. There's an expectation that the environment will improve as well as the overall perception of the organization. To produce the desired results, there is a certain amount of pushing and nudging the community by the CEO that takes place. Therefore, the correlation between the community's capacity for pushing and nudging, and the tenure of the chief executive officer, can be direct. At some point capacity is reached and a change is desired. The silver lining is that if the programmatic activities that resulted from the pushing and nudging were successful, the organization is in a better place, and the executive can move to the next "assignment."

It's imperative that the CEO is aware of the evolution of leadership as well as community norms. As discussed earlier, the CEO has the responsibility to understand the pulse of the community, and especially the pulse of the organization's volunteer leadership. There is a need for the CEO to process a "sixth sense" sensitivity to changes in perception relative to programmatic activities as well as changes in perception that are related directly to the CEO. The development of this skill is both intuitive and learned. It involves always having eyes and ears wide open to notice ever so slight changes in behavior. Being aware of long-time supporters who start to become distant and begin to appear not as supportive. An increase in the scrutiny of new programs or activities being introduced, or an increase in the scrutiny of the performance of existing programs or activities, are all signs of leadership evolution. Also, you should be aware of "meetings after the meeting" or huddling among members. The ultimate sign that something is not right is to have your leadership convene a meeting without you being invited or go into an executive session without you being present or knowing what's on the agenda. If you are not in the meeting, then more than likely, <u>you</u> are the agenda.

It's believed that most CEOs are released from duty months or even years from the time leadership started discussing making a change. This is due to the reluctance of leadership to move on such a major undertaking as replacing the head of the organization. It's sometimes easier for the current chair to kick the can down the road and let the issue soon become the next chair's problem. Replacing the CEO requires communicating with and assuring all stakeholders and funders that that the organization is stable and sustainable. An open and candid conversation with the remaining staff is also needed to calm their anxiety and secure their commitment to ensuring a sustainable transition period. This is a huge responsibility for a part-time volunteer (Chapter 6), who in most cases has a full-time job.

If you are ever called into a meeting and released and you were totally surprised shame on you. You have been sleeping at the wheel and totally unaware of what's going on around you. Open your eyes and be aware of changes and behaviors among your leadership and stakeholders, as well as your community.

The Bloomberg quote above relates to the leader realizing that some battles need to be transitioned to someone else. It's the realization that you have no personal desire to continue fighting an issue that is too important to the community not to be addressed. Therefore, it's time to go. There is no reason to feel ashamed or defeated because it's a noble decision. You have placed the community's interest above your own. Hold your head up and prepare for the next opportunity.

KEY TAKEAWAY:

Entering the arena of non-profit CEO means you will have a tenure based on the evolution of your various 'communities' and stakeholders. It is important to remain ever-vigilant to the state of your relationships both inside and outside of your organization. Proactively solicit feedback and keep your eyes on what's bubbling up under the water. Be prepared to know when your time of service and impact has peaked and should come to a close, and then ensure a positive transition for both you and your organization.

Chapter Thirteen

"Hail! Hail! The Gang's All Here"

"If you fulfill the wishes of your employees, the employees will fulfill your visions." **Amit Kalantri**

Throughout my working career, I've heard that we are only as good as the people around us. Although it might sound like a something good to say, trust me, it isn't. There is a direct correlation between the quality of the team you place around you and the quality of the performance of the organization, as well as how you and the organization are perceived among your leadership and in the community. Regardless of the size of your team, there is never a reason to compromise on the quality of the individuals you hire. You should "hire long and fire short." Take the time to match the right person to the job description and attempt to ensure that the candidate is a cultural fit for you and the organization.

Your employees are not your friends. They, along with you, are members of the team, who've come together to collectively execute the mission of the organization. As CEO, your responsibility is to facilitate a culture of support and respect that inspires every team member to give 100 percent. The ideal team member is a self-motivated craft master who possesses passion for the organization's mission and their role in executing the mission. Your commitment should always be to have their backs and be willing to step in and take the heat when necessary. For me, the buck stops in my office, and my entire team knows it. My team knew that from me they would receive praise in public and when necessary, discipline in private. And more importantly, every team member knows that I will not hesitate to initiate separation when necessary. Hire long and fire short.

I personally do not believe in micro-managing, nor do I have the time, but my door is always open to all team members. Theoretically, every activity undertaken by the organization should directly or indirectly impact the mission. Therefore, every activity is in some way connected to the CEO, regardless of the organizational chart. If a team member needs a few minutes with me to bring clarity to an issue, the quicker we can make that happen, the better it will be for the organization and all involved.

A lot has been written about loyalty between an employer and an employee. Peter K. Murdock, V.P. of Recruiting for Blackmon Mooring / BMS CAT, penned an article in the December 28, 2017 issue of *Forbes* titled, "*The New Reality of Employee Loyalty.*" In the article he notes three keys to retaining top performers: (1) Know your employee value proposition (EVP) for each role and make sure it aligns with the employees in that role. (2) Make sure that employee reviews include time spent understanding how employees see their own careers developing. (3) <u>Know upfront that three years is long-term planning for your employees</u> and preparing accordingly is imperative. The workplace is substantially different from when I entered it more that forty years ago. CEOs that work towards understanding the current environment will realize a higher probability of building success and sustaining a cohesive and productive team.

KEY TAKEAWAY:

Your position as CEO brings major responsibilities in terms of ensuring a collaborative, constructive and productive team. It also means that 'people issues' in the organization all come back to you and your leadership. Hiring smart is one of the most important roles and challenges you will have- it can also be one of the costliest in terms of impact on your success and your bottom line. Be open, be honest, be available and be professional in all of your work relationships.

Chapter 14

You are Your Brother's Keeper

"There's a destiny that makes us brothers, none goes his way alone. All that you send into the lives of others, comes back into your own."
Edwin Markham

Throughout my thirty-plus year chamber of commerce and economic development career, I've always considered my role to be that of a community servant. I've had the fortunate opportunity to be associated with four organizations in four great cities. My first not-for-profit job was with the Chamber of Commerce in my hometown of Shreveport, LA. I became intimately involved with making the city and region a better place to live and since Shreveport was my hometown, I was personally invested. The passion for the city and its plight was not new to me and it was easy for me to define my job as one of community service.

Based on my experience in Shreveport, I carried the community service mantra with me to St. Louis, Pittsburg and Charlotte. I truly believe that accepting the fact that I am my brother's keeper, and that my role in those respective cities was one of service, made me a better leader and a better person. I have shared with my team members in all four cities that our mission is a calling, not a job. And I made it clear that if you are here only for the opportunity to have employment, and you process no emotional attachment to our mission or to the people we serve, then you might be in the wrong place.

I find personal joy in knowing that the fruits of our labor directly improve the quality of life for the citizens we serve. There is no better feeling than driving by a building that had been vacant for years and see a once empty parking lot now filled with cars. Cars belonging to men and women who now have sustainable employment and knowing that you had something to do with it. If the organization's mission, goals and objectives are crafted with a community service focus, every resource expended should be directed at making the community better. Making the community a place where the citizens are proud to call it home because they know someone cares allows us to tolerate the negative issues I discussed earlier, because we understand that there's a higher purpose for the work that we do.

This quote by Edwin Markham is one of my favorites. I've lived my life believing that if I treat my brothers and sisters the way I would like to be treated, I will receive the treatment I desire. I've made that belief a part of my professional career and through the years have reaped the benefits. I can attest, without hesitation that my career and my life have both greatly benefitted from the way I treat and interact with the people around me. The servant approach has made my life gratifying and rewarding on so many fronts, and I'm very grateful. I hope that those reading this will seek and find the same joy.

KEY TAKEAWAY:

It is an amazing thing, being the CEO of a not-for-profit organization. Amazing because it is more than a job, position or career. It truly is a calling. It's an opportunity to make a lasting positive impact on your community and for the greater good.

Seize your opportunity where your heart, head, skills, talents and passions lead you and you will leave a legacy.

SUMMARY

Completing this book is the fulfillment of a life-long dream. I hope that the tips offered can pave the way for a smooth and long tenure wherever you may be employed.

Special thanks to content editors Dean Whitaker, Tim Chase and Dianne L. Chase (no relation) as well as grammar and style editors Ellery Turner and my daughter, Ronda Bryant, for their assistance and thoughtful advice.

I would appreciate receiving your thoughts or comments. I can be reached at Ronnie@RLBryantLLC.com.

Peace!!

Quotes

"Risk more than others think is safe. Care more than others think is wise. Dream more than others think is practical. Expect more than others think is possible." Claude Bissell

"Leaders must be tough enough to fight, tender enough to cry, human enough to make mistakes, humble enough to admit them, strong enough to absorb the pain, and resilient enough to bounce back and keep moving." Jesse Jackson

"Good business leaders create a vision, articulate the vision, passionately own the vision, and relentlessly drive it to completion." Jack Welch

"Patience is the ability to idle your motor when you feel like stripping your gears." Barbara Johnson

"A leader takes people where they want to go. A great leader takes people where they don't necessarily want to go, but ought to be." Rosalynn Carter

"Only to the extent that trustees give support when it is needed does the chief executive want a strong board." Robert Greenleaf

"The world isn't interested in the storms you encountered, but whether or not you brought in the ship." Raul Armesto

"When I look in the mirror each morning, I accept the fact that at least 30% of the contacts I make will not be in agreement with me." Ronnie Bryant

"If you don't see yourself as a winner, then you cannot perform as a winner." Zig Ziglar

"Integrity is doing the right thing, when no one is watching." C.S. Lewis

"The minute you stop making decisions to do your job and start making decisions to keep your job, you have become worthless." Ronnie Bryant

"You know it's time to leave when you begin to believe something can't be done." Michael Bloomberg
"If you fulfill the wishes of your employees, the employees will fulfill your visions." Amit Kalantri

"There's a destiny that makes us brothers; none goes his way along. All that you send into the lives of others, comes back into your own." Edwin Markham

KEY CHAPTER TAKEAWAYS

Chapter 1

Serving as a CEO for a not-for-profit organization comes with unique challenges. Be prepared to spend more time communicating with influencers and internal stakeholders than you may have done in previous roles. Be proactive in setting clear objectives for your performance and that of your organization.

Chapter 2

As the CEO of a non-profit organization your leadership encompasses two strategic approaches - that of the dynamic thought leader and that of a servant leader. Your thought leadership must embody strength, vision, and drive, while your servant leadership must embrace and navigate divergent positions and personalities to move forward toward collective success.

Chapter 3

It is imperative that you establish a clear vision for what success looks like for your organization. The vision is your roadmap and guiding star as you drive the road to reaching your goals. You must get your stakeholders on your 'vision bus' from the start and then move ahead with your tactical plan and execution.

Chapter 4

Remember you are the 'brand' for your organization, especially when it comes to taking a public stand and/or making public comments. Learn to carefully consider the impact of your words and know when and how to respond on issues, both internally and externally. The most successful leaders have on-going professional communication training.

Chapter 5

As the CEO of a not-for-profit you must be the driving force, but in a way that engenders support for your leadership and your vision. The key is to build understanding, professional respect and support with your core leadership. Maintaining professional and, to a very measured extent, personal relationships- with a keen eye on any individual 'agendas' - will help you keep a steady hand on the backseat wheel.

Chapter 6

One of your key responsibilities in being an effective CEO is to clearly understand the individuals in your core leadership, including why they committed to being a director and their view of where they see the organization going and why. In addition, you have the critical role of providing clear, consistent information so that they may feel fully informed and enabled to successfully carry out their roles as board members.

Chapter 7

As the leader of your organization you will have a myriad of stakeholders who have their own constituencies, opinions, agendas and biases. It will take your skills in emotional intelligence and collaborative engagement to bring alignment for the vision you have set. It is important that you proactively communicate with these decision makers in order to drive cohesion and cooperation.

Chapter 8

One of the keys to maintaining leadership is to remember that you are in the people business. Just as with public relations, you should spend the greater percentage of your time on solidifying relationships with your supporters and your 'middle of the roaders' rather than trying to pull the constant detractors to your side. As the old saying goes - "You can please some of the people all of the time, you can please all of the people some of the time, but you can't please all of the people all of the time." Don't take it personally.

Chapter 9

Before ever stepping into the role of CEO it is nothing short of critical for you to believe with every fiber of your being in the mission, vision, values, purpose and potential of the organization. Anything short of that is a recipe for failure. Your stakeholders will know —sooner or later- if you do not fully have your heart and soul in what you do, whether you embody the organization's best interests, and if you truly are walking your talk when it comes to your commitment to their success.

Chapter 10

You, as CEO, drive the culture of an organization. Both personally and professionally you must represent —and Model - the highest standards of conduct and behavior. Maintaining unimpeachable ethical standards is not an option. Creating an environment that fosters transparency, collaboration and collegiately is under your purview. Your responsibility is to build and nurture your teams for a positive and productive working environment.

Chapter 11

As the leader of your organization, with non-stop demands, duties and expectations, it is important to maintain your mental, physical and emotional health in order to succeed. That means thinking long and hard about how you will prioritize your life in terms of work and personal commitments. You must decide early on how you will create balance to prevent burnout. Preserving quality of life in and out of the workplace is important for success on both fronts.

Chapter 12

Entering the arena of non-profit CEO means you will have a tenure based on the evolution of your various 'communities' and stakeholders. It is important to remain ever-vigilant to the state of your relationships both inside and outside of your organization. Proactively solicit feedback and keep your eyes on what's bubbling up under the water. Be prepared to know when your time of service and impact has peaked and should come to a close, and then ensure a positive transition for both you and your organization.

Chapter 13

Your position as CEO brings major responsibilities in terms of ensuring a collaborative, constructive and productive team. It also means that 'people issues' in the organization all come back to you and your leadership. Hiring smart is one of the most important roles and challenges you will have- it can also be one of the costliest in terms of impact on your success and your bottom line. Be open, be honest, be available and be professional in all of your work relationships.

Chapter 14

It is an amazing thing, being the CEO of a not-for-profit organization. Amazing because it is more than a job, position or career. It truly is a calling. It's an opportunity to make a lasting positive impact on your community and for the greater good. Seize your opportunity where your heart, head, skills, talents and passions lead you and you will leave a legacy.

About the Author

Ronnie L. Bryant is founder and principal consultant at Ronnie L. Bryant, LLC, a consulting firm specializing in executive coaching, organizational management, and board development and training for top-level corporate and not-for-profit managers. Bryant created the company in 2017 to help executives improve their leadership skills and business acumen to operate organizations while maintaining a competitive edge in diverse, evolving domestic and global marketplaces.

Prior to forming Ronnie L. Bryant, LLC, Bryant served as President and CEO of Charlotte Regional Partnership in North Carolina, for over thirteen years. Bryant and his team marketed the sixteen-county region to domestic and global companies as the premier site for expansion and relocation. He created strategic partnerships and brokered viable collaborations, which earned him a national reputation for creating and implementing effective economic development programs.

Bryant's leadership in economic development spans thirty-five years, including executive positions at Greater Shreveport Chamber of Commerce (Louisiana), St. Louis Regional Chamber & Growth Association (Missouri), and Pittsburgh Regional Alliance (Pennsylvania). Bryant quickly became one of the nation's most sought-after economic developers, piquing the interests of Charlotte business leaders, who hired him to lead Charlotte Regional Partnership in 2005.

Since his appointment, Bryant has served in the Charlotte business community as a board director for American Leadership Forum, Aspire Community Capital, Goodwill Industries of the Southern Piedmont, Charlotte City Club, and Jazz Arts Initiative. Bryant is a national board member for The Bollinger Foundation (Washington, D.C.) and The Institute for Work and the Economy (Illinois). He was a board member for The Federal Reserve Bank of Cleveland Pittsburgh Branch.

Additionally, Bryant is a past chairman for International Economic Development Council and a member of Southern Economic Developers Council, among other associations. He is a former dean and a faculty member for University of Oklahoma's Economic Development Institute as well as an adjunct professor for University of North Carolina at Charlotte.

Bryant earned a B.S. in business management from Louisiana State University in Shreveport. He was a fellow at The Center for Intentional Leadership®, Center for Creative Leadership, Northwestern University Kellogg School of Management, and University of Oklahoma's Economic Development Institute. Bryant is a recipient of the American Economic Development Council's Robert B. Cassell Leadership Award.

Throughout his career, Bryant has garnered national recognition and top industry ranking for his leadership by *Site Selection* magazine, *Pittsburgh Post-Gazette*, and *Charlotte Magazine*. He is an acclaimed contributor to and global lecturer in economic development marketing, organizational governance, strategic management, and current trends in civic and community engagement.

www.ingramcontent.com/pod-product-compliance
Lightning Source LLC
Chambersburg PA
CBHW030735180526
45157CB00008BA/3177